The Bread Baking Cookbook for Beginners

100 Simple and Delicious Bread Machine Recipes Anyone Can Make.

Ava Thomas

© COPYRIGHT 2022 ALL RIGHTS RESERVED

This document is geared towards providing exact and reliable information concerning the topic and issue covered. The publication is sold with the idea that the publisher is not required to render accounting, officially permitted or otherwise qualified services. If advice is necessary, legal or professional, a practiced individual in the profession should be ordered.

In no way is it legal to reproduce, duplicate, or transmit any part of this document in either electronic means or printed format. Recording this publication is strictly prohibited, and any storage of this document is not allowed unless with written permission from the publisher. All rights reserved.

Warning Disclaimer, the information in this book is true and complete to the best of our knowledge. All recommendation is made without guarantee on the part of the author or story publishing. The author and publisher disclaim and liability in connection with the use of this information

Table of Contents

INTRODUCTION 9

BAKE BREAD RECIPES 10

   1. Turmeric curry bread with black sesame seeds 10

   2. baguette 12

   3. Banana bread with walnuts 15

   4. Corn bread from the pan 18

   5. Crunchy buttermilk bread 21

   6. Walnut bread 23

   7. banana bread 25

   8. Rye bread with sourdough 27

   9. Hearty sourdough rye bread 29

   10. Mexican corn bread 31

   11. Tomato bread sticks 33

   12. Garlic bread sticks 35

   13. Potato focaccia with zucchini 38

   14. Grilled focaccia 41

   15. Quick spelled bread 43

   16. Spicy party pizza bread 45

   17. Pumpkin seed bread 47

18. Sweet potato bread 49

19. Spice bread 52

20. Mixed bread 54

GRILLED BREADS 56

21. Bread on a skewer 56

22. garlic bread 58

23. Grilled toasted bread 60

24. Bread on a stick 62

25. Baked herb bread 64

26. Filled white bread 67

27. Walnut bread 69

28. Striploin steak with garlic bread 71

29. Low carb focaccia 73

30. Grill flatbread 76

31. Spicy grilled bread 78

32. Herbal baguette 80

33. Spicy bread on the grill 82

34. Suckling Pig Sandwich 84

35. Crispy bread and cheese salad 86

36. Turkey cream cheese rolls 89

37. Cevapcici in flatbread 91

38. Breads with smoked salmon 92

39. Gratinated bread 95
40. Small Flatbreads 96

BREAD FOR BREAKFAST 98
41. Fitness bread 98
42. Cocoa and Orange Bread 100
43. Whole meal spelled bread 103
44. Herb egg bread with tomato cream 105
45. Kamut bread with oats and millet 108
46. Fitness bread with smoked trout 110
47. Fried egg in crispy bread 112
48. Tramezzini with tuna 114
49. Olive bread 116
50. Brightened banana bread 118
51. Microwave bread 120
52. Creamy Cucumber Sandwiches 122
53. Fluffy Protein Bread With Nutri-Plus 124
54. Microwave Quick Keto Bread 126
55. Cheese bread with bacon 127
56. Cheese Halibut Cheese Bread 129
57. Grilled Eggplant Sandwich 131

58. Cucumber and kale open sandwich 133
59. Spinach Cheese Bread 135
60. Tramezzini with ham and gorgonzola 137

SNACKS 139

61. Gratinated bread 139
62. Bread cheese skewers 141
63. Herbal bread terrine with currant 143
64. Kamut bread with oats and millet 145
65. Ham sandwich 147
66. Bruschette with egg topping 150
67. Tramezzini with tuna 151
68. potato bread 153
69. Avocado bread 156
70. Olive bread 158
71. Eggplant cream on spelled buckwheat bread 160
72. Crispy fish bread 163
73. Onion bread with goat cheese 166
74. Bruschetta with herbs 168
75. Baked avocado baguette 170
76. Baked baguette with salmon and horseradish 172
77. Bruschetta with Tomatoes 174
78. Sandwich cake 176

79. Tuna toast with pesto 178

80. Bruschette with olive topping 180

SALAD RECIPES 182

81. Panzanella (Tuscan Bread Salad) 182

82. Tomato bread salad with baked calamaretti 184

83. White bread salad with mozzarella 187

84. Baked bread salad with dried tomatoes from the hot air fryer 189

85. Tomato bread salad with fried pulpo 191

86. bread salad 194

87. Tomato bread salad with baked calamaretti 196

88. Bread salad with beans and peppers 198

89. taramosalata 200

90. Italian bread salad 202

91. Crispy bread and cheese salad 204

92. Cevapcici in flatbread 207

93. Fluffy Protein Bread With Nutri-Plus 209

94. Colorful layered salad 211

95. Caprese sandwich 213

96. Baked eggplant parmesan in the leaf pan 215

97. Grilled Eggplant Sandwich 217

98. Herb egg bread with tomato cream 219

99. Mediterranean toasts 222

100. Tramezzini with egg and anchovies 223

CONCLUSION 225

INTRODUCTION

Bread is a food that is present in the diet of most people around the world. Although very popular, you can find different versions of this food and each country has its own favorites.

In addition to the wide variety of breads we can find, it is possible to serve this food at any time of the day for breakfast, lunch, light meals and even dinner.

We don't always feel like going to a bakery and want to eat hot bread made at home. Or even want to eat bread that is not easy to buy ready-made. To solve these problems, you can prepare delicious bread in the comfort of your own home.

BAKE BREAD RECIPES

1. Turmeric curry bread with black sesame seeds

ingredients

- 150 g Cashew nuts
- 1 teaspoon Dry yeast
- 400 g Wheat flour type 550
- 10 g butter ☐ 3 tsp sugar
- 2 teaspoons salt
- 2 g Cumin/cumin
- 1 g Turmeric powder
- 2 g Curry powder
- 1 of the black sesame

Preparation steps
1. Finely chop the cashew nuts. Add yeast, flour, butter, sugar, salt, cumin, turmeric and curry powder to the pan of the bread maker.
2. Add 280 ml of water and bake bread in the bread maker. Cut into the bread 1 hour before the end of the baking time and sprinkle with sesame seeds.

2. baguette

ingredients
- 250 g wheat flour type 550
- 225 g whole wheat flour
- 15 g fresh yeast
- 12 g salt (2 teaspoons)
- 1 tbsp rapeseed oil

Preparation steps
1. The evening before, for the starter dough, put 125 g wheat flour and 75 g whole wheat flour in a bowl. Crumble in 10 g of yeast and add 250 ml of lukewarm water.
2. Knead with the dough hook of the hand mixer for 1 minute. Cover well with cling film

and let rise at room temperature for at least 12 hours.
3. The next day, put the rest of the flour and the rest of the whole wheat flour in a bowl with salt and make a well in the middle. Crumble in the rest of the yeast. Pour in 125 ml of lukewarm water and let it rest for 10 minutes.
4. Add the pre-dough to the other ingredients in the bowl and knead everything with the dough hook of the hand mixer for 4 minutes.
5. Place the dough on a floured work surface and knead by hand for another 10 minutes, adding a little flour if necessary, until the dough no longer sticks to the hands.
6. Put the oil in a bowl and turn the ball of dough in it to moisten the surface. Cover with cling film and let rise at room temperature for 1 1/2 hours until the volume has doubled.
7. Lightly beat the dough together and shape into an elongated loaf. Let rise for another 60 minutes.

8. Place the dough piece on the floured work surface and quarter.
9. Bring the dough pieces into baguette sticks by gently pressing and rolling them at the same time.
10. Place the baguette dough pieces on a baking sheet lined with baking paper and cover with a floured kitchen towel and let rise for 40 minutes.
11. Score the baguettes diagonally several times with a very sharp knife. Bake in the preheated oven at 220 ° C on the 2nd rack from the bottom for 30-35 minutes.
12. Let the baguettes cool on the oven shelf before serving.

3. Banana bread with walnuts

ingredients
- 300 g wheat flour type 1050
- 1 packet baking powder
- ½ tsp salt
- nutmeg
- 150 g walnut kernels
- 1 vanilla pod
- 1 apple
- 80 g butter

- 50 g coconut blossom sugar
- 1 egg
- 500 g ripe bananas (3 ripe bananas)

Preparation steps
1. Sift the flour, baking powder, and salt into a mixing bowl. Rub some nutmeg directly into it.
2. Finely chop walnuts in a lightning chopper or with a large knife and add to the flour mixture.
3. Peel the bananas, cut them into small pieces, place in a bowl and puree with a hand blender or finely mash them with a fork.
4. Cut the vanilla pod lengthways, scrape out the pulp and stir into the banana sauce.
5. Wash and grate the apple and stir in the butter and coconut blossom sugar in a bowl with the whisk of a hand mixer until foamy, stir in the egg. Then gradually add the banana puree and flour mixture to the butter mixture.
6. Grease a small loaf pan if necessary. Pour in the dough and smooth it out with a rubber spatula.
7. Bake in the preheated oven at 175 ° C on the middle shelf for 50-60 minutes. Stick a

wooden skewer in the middle of the cake: if it stays clean when you pull it out, the cake is done; otherwise bake for a few more minutes.
8. Take the finished bread out of the oven, let it cool down in the baking pan for 5 minutes, then turn it out.

4. Corn bread from the pan

ingredients

- ½ fret sage
- 50 walnut kernels
- 150 g corn grits
- 100 g wheat flour type 1050
- 1 tbsp baking powder
- 1 tsp salt
- 250 ml milk (1.5% fat)

- 2 tbsp honey
- 2 eggs
- 90 g butter

Preparation steps

1. Wash the sage, shake dry, pluck the leaves, put 6 large ones aside. Roughly chop the remaining sage and walnuts each.
2. Mix the corn grits, flour, baking powder and salt in a bowl with the chopped sage.
3. Mix milk, honey and eggs in a small bowl.
4. Heat an ovenproof pan in the oven preheated to 200 ° C for 10 minutes. Melt the butter in it.
5. Pour the melted butter into the egg-milk except for about 2 tbsp. Put the sage leaves in the hot pan.
6. Stir egg milk into the flour mixture to make a smooth batter. Pour 1/4 of it into the pan and swirl to distribute it.

7. Scatter chopped walnuts on top and top with the rest of the batter. Put the pan back in the oven and bake the cornbread for 18-20 minutes. Then remove the pan, let it cool for 10 minutes and turn the cornbread out onto a platter.

5. Crunchy buttermilk bread

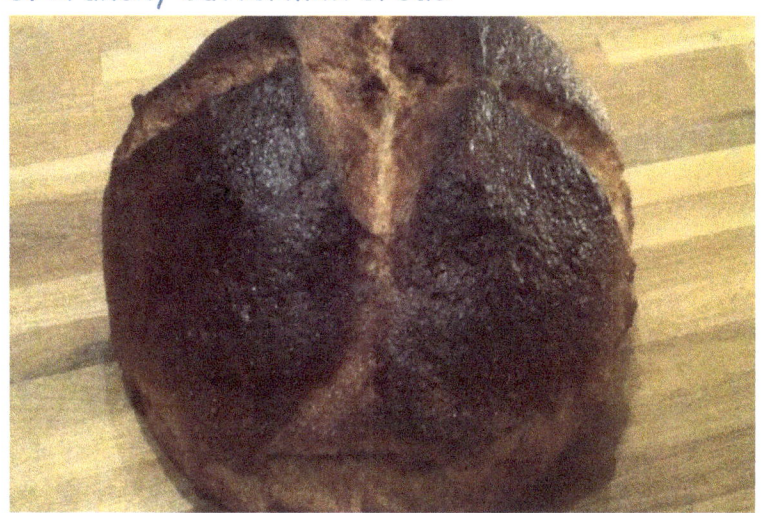

ingredients
- 100 g nut muesli
- 250 ml buttermilk
- 300 g wheat flour type 1050
- 150 g whole meal semolina
- 1 packet tartar baking powder
- nutmeg
- 600 g bananas (4 small, ripe bananas)
- ½ lime
- 80 g honey

Preparation steps
1. Mix the muesli and buttermilk in a bowl, leave to soak for about 10 minutes.
2. In the meantime, mix the flour, semolina and baking powder in a second bowl, rub in a pinch of nutmeg.
3. Peel the bananas and mash them with a fork.
4. Squeeze half a lime.
5. Add the banana puree, honey, 1 tbsp lime juice and the muesli-buttermilk mixture to the flour mixture. Knead everything with the dough hook of the hand mixer to a juicy dough.
6. Place the dough in a loaf pan (30 cm long) lined with baking paper and bake on the oven shelf in a preheated oven at 200 ° C for about 40 minutes.

6. Walnut bread

ingredients
- 500 g whole wheat flour
- 1 packet dry yeast
- 10 g whole cane sugar (1 teaspoon)
- 2 branches rosemary
- 150 g walnut kernels
- 2 tbsp honey
- 1 tsp salt
- pepper
- 50 ml milk (1.5% fat)
- 50 ml olive oil

Preparation steps
1. Mix the flour, yeast and sugar in a mixing bowl.
2. Stir in 250 ml of lukewarm water with the dough hook of the hand mixer until a uniform dough has formed. Cover and let rise in a warm place for about 30 minutes.
3. In the meantime, rinse off the rosemary, shake dry, pluck needles and chop.
4. Briefly toast the walnuts in a non-stick pan. Mix in the honey and rosemary and heat. Season with salt and pepper and place on a plate.
5. Heat the milk lukewarm, then stir into the dough with the oil. Knead in the nut-honey mixture until everything has bonded and the dough is shiny and smooth.
6. Shape the dough into a long loaf of bread and place on a baking sheet lined with baking paper. Cover and let rise in a warm place for about 20 minutes. Bake in the preheated oven at 220 ° C on the middle shelf for approx. 40 minutes.

7. banana bread

ingredients

- 100 g hazelnut kernels
- 600 g ripe bananas (4 ripe bananas)
- 100 ml rapeseed oil
- 70 ml maple syrup
- 1 pinch cinnamon powder
- 1 pinch nutmeg powder
- 1 pinch salt
- 40 ml oat drink (oat milk) (4 tbsp)
- 280 g wholemeal spelled flour

- ½ packet baking powder
- 40 g ground almond kernels (2 tbsp)

Preparation steps
1. Roughly chop the hazelnuts and set aside. Peel and chop the bananas and chop them up with a fork or hand blender.
2. Beat the bananas together with oil, maple syrup, cinnamon, nutmeg, salt and oat drink with a hand mixer until creamy. Sieve flour with baking powder and mix into the banana mixture. Then fold in the almonds and half of the nuts.
3. Pour the dough into a loaf pan lined with baking paper and sprinkle with the remaining hazelnuts. Bake in a preheated oven at 180 ° C for about 50-60 minutes until golden brown.

8. Rye bread with sourdough

ingredients
- 1 bag liquid natural sourdough
- ½ level tsp aniseed
- ½ level tsp fennel seeds
- ½ level tsp coriander seeds
- ½ level tsp caraway seeds
- 400 g spelled flour type 1050
- 400 g whole meal rye flour
- 2 packages dry yeast
- 1 tsp raw cane sugar

- 2 tsp salt

Preparation steps
1. Heat the sourdough bag in a bowl with lukewarm water for about 15 minutes. Meanwhile, finely crush the anise, fennel, coriander and caraway seeds in a mortar.
2. Mix both types of flour, yeast, sugar and salt in a bowl. Add about 400 ml of lukewarm water and sourdough to the mixture and knead everything well. If necessary, add a little lukewarm water or flour.
3. Cover the dough in a bowl and let rise in a warm place for about 1 hour.
4. Then knead the dough well again and work in the bread spice. Put the dough in a floured proofing basket, cover and let rise for 1-2 hours.
5. Line a baking sheet with parchment paper and top it with rye bread. Bake rye bread with a dash of water in a preheated oven at 240 ° C for 10 minutes, then bake at 200 ° C in 35-40 minutes (knock test).
6. Take rye bread out of the oven and let cool down completely.

9. Hearty sourdough rye bread

ingredients

1 tsp honey

450 g wholemeal rye flour

200 g whole wheat flour

1 ½ tsp salt

1 tsp ground coriander seeds

1 pinch ground caraway seeds

1 packet dry yeast

Preparation steps

For the sourdough, mix together 250 ml of warm water and honey, add 150 g of wholemeal rye flour and mix with a wooden spoon to form a smooth dough. Cover the bowl and let it stand in a warm place at at least 20 ° C for three days; Stir vigorously in the morning and in the evening: the mixture ferments, forms bubbles and the volume increases. The finished dough should be thick, smell freshly sour and bubble.

Then mix both types of flour with salt, spices, sourdough and yeast. Add 250 ml of lukewarm water and knead everything into an elastic dough. Cover and let rise in a warm place for about 1 hour. Take the dough out of the bowl, knead vigorously on a floured work surface and shape into a round loaf.

Cover the loaf in a floured proving basket and let rise for another 30 minutes at room temperature. Place on a baking sheet lined with baking paper, brush with water and cut into if necessary. Bake in a preheated oven at 220 ° C for 10 minutes, then bake at 180 ° C in 45 minutes; Open the oven door slightly after 35 minutes.

10. Mexican corn bread

ingredients
- 2 red chili peppers
- 6th jalapeños (glass)
- 50 g butter
- 200 g whole wheat flour
- 1 packet baking powder
- salt
- 325 g corn grits
- 500 ml buttermilk
- 50 g liquid honey
- 2 eggs

- 1 tbsp rapeseed oil

Preparation steps
1. Halve the chili peppers lengthways, remove the core, wash and chop.
2. Finely chop the jalapeños. Melt the butter and let it cool down a bit.
3. Sift the flour, baking powder and 1 teaspoon salt into a bowl and mix with the corn grits.
4. Mix the buttermilk, honey, eggs and melted butter together.
5. Add to the flour together with the chillies and jalapeños and stir everything into a smooth batter.
6. Brush a 30 cm long loaf pan with oil and pour in the dough. Bake in the preheated oven on the 2nd shelf from the bottom on an oven rack at 180 ° C for 35-40 minutes.
7. Let the cornbread cool in the tin for 10 minutes, then turn it out onto an oven rack and let it cool completely. Cornbread tastes simply coated with butter, but is also a good accompaniment to chilies and stews.

11. Tomato bread sticks

ingredients
- 250 g whole wheat flour
- 250 g whole meal spelled flour
- 1 ½ packet dry yeast
- 1 tsp whole cane sugar
- 1 tsp salt
- 100 g dried tomatoes (pickled in oil)
- 100 ml tomato juice
- 5 stems thyme

Preparation steps
1. Mix both types of flour, yeast, sugar and salt in a mixing bowl.
2. Drain the tomatoes, collecting 1 tablespoon of oil. To dice tomatoes.
3. Heat the tomato juice and 250 ml water in a saucepan lukewarm.
4. Add the tomato water and the collected tomato oil to the flour and knead with the dough hook of the hand mixer until the dough bubbles.
5. Cover and let rise in a warm place for about 30 minutes.
6. Wash the thyme, shake dry and pluck the leaves off.
7. Knead tomato cubes and thyme leaves into the dough. Shape the dough into 2 short breadsticks.
8. Place on a baking sheet lined with baking paper, score with a knife and let rise for another 10 minutes. Bake in a preheated oven at 200 ° C for 25-30 minutes.

12. Garlic bread sticks

ingredients

- 1 cube yeast (42 g)
- 150 ml olive oil
- 2 tsp fine sea salt
- 1 tbsp honey
- 700 g spelled flour type 1050
- 300 g wholemeal spelled flour
- 4 fresh cloves of garlic
- 1 branch rosemary
- 60 g grated Emmentaler

Preparation steps

1. Prepare all ingredients and let them reach room temperature.
2. Crumble the yeast in a bowl and add approx. 650 ml of lukewarm water. Mix with 80 ml of oil, salt and honey until the yeast has completely dissolved. Pour the flour into a bowl and make a hollow in the middle. Pour in the yeast mixture and knead everything from the center to a firm dough. Place the dough on the floured work surface and knead until the dough is smooth and pliable. Possibly work in a little more flour so that the dough no longer sticks. Put in a bowl and cover in a warm place and let rise for about 45 minutes.
3. Peel the garlic and chop in to fine slithers. Wash the rosemary, shake dry, pluck and finely chop. Mix with the garlic and 4 tablespoons of olive oil.
4. Knead the dough well again on a floured work surface and quarter it. Shape each quarter into a long strand and gently press flat. Brush with the garlic oil and twist into a braid beginning in the middle. Press the ends together well and place the bread on a

baking sheet lined with baking paper. Brush with the rest of the oil and sprinkle with the cheese and bake in a preheated oven at 220 ° C for about 20 minutes until golden brown.

13. Potato focaccia with zucchini

ingredients

- 200 g waxy potatoes (2 waxy potatoes)
- ½ cube yeast
- 1 tsp honey
- salt
- 6 tbsp olive oil
- 105 g wholemeal spelled flour
- 200 g spelled flour (type 630)
- ½ zucchini
- 1 shallot
- 1 ½ tsp coarse sea salt
- 1 pinch chili powder
- 1 pinch pepper
- 30 g capers (3 tbsp)

Preparation steps

1. Cover and cook the potatoes in boiling water over a low heat for 30 minutes until soft. Drain, let cool for 5 minutes, peel and chop with a pounder.

2. Whisk the yeast with honey, a little salt, 2 tablespoons of oil and 120 ml of lukewarm water, add to the mashed potatoes and stir to a homogeneous mass, then mix in 300 g of flour. Let rise in a warm place for at least 60 minutes.

3. Knead the dough on a floured work surface and cut in half. Roll out both dough balls into focaccia flatbreads, place on a baking sheet lined with baking paper and let rise again for 30 minutes.

4. In the meantime, clean and wash the zucchini, peel the shallot, cut both into slices and mix with the sea salt, chilli, pepper and 2 tablespoons of oil. Press with your fingers

into the focaccia wells and distribute the vegetable mixture in it, cover with capers and drizzle with the remaining oil.
5. Bake the focaccia in a preheated oven at 180 ° C for about 25 minutes until golden brown.

14. Grilled focaccia

ingredients

- ½ cube yeast
- 1 tsp agave syrup
- 500 g whole wheat flour
- 1 tsp salt
- 1 clove of garlic
- 2 branches rosemary
- 2 tbsp olive oil

Preparation steps
1. Crumble the yeast in a small bowl and pour agave syrup over it. Set aside, about 10 minutes, until the yeast has dissolved and starts to bubble.
2. Put the flour and salt in a bowl. Add yeast and 300 ml of lukewarm water and work into a smooth dough. Add a little more water if necessary. Cover the dough and let it rest for about 2 hours.
3. In the meantime, press on the garlic clove. Pluck the rosemary needles from the branches. Heat the olive oil in a pan, let the garlic and rosemary steep for 10 minutes over a low heat.
4. Divide the dough into four roughly equal portions and shape into oval dough cakes with your hands on a lightly floured work surface. Brush the dough with the rosemary oil and grill on the grill with the lid closed for 3-4 minutes.

15. Quick spelled bread

ingredients
- 1 cube yeast
- 1 tsp salt
- 4 tbsp apple cider vinegar
- 500 g wholemeal spelled flour
- 150 g kernels, nuts or seeds to taste (e.g. walnuts, hazelnuts and pumpkin seeds)
- 1 tsp butter (5 g)

Preparation steps
1. Dissolve the yeast in 500 ml of lukewarm water. Add salt and vinegar and stir until all the ingredients have dissolved.
2. Put the flour in a bowl and mix in 130 g of seeds. Pour in the yeast water and mix everything with the dough hook of the food processor or the electric hand mixer to form a smooth dough. The dough is sticky and relatively moist.
3. Grease a loaf pan (30 cm long) with the butter and pour in the batter. Cover with a damp kitchen towel and let rise in a warm, draftfree place for about 20 minutes.
4. In the meantime, preheat the oven to 200 °C (convection).
5. When the surface of the dough begins to curve upwards, sprinkle the remaining seeds over the bread and bake in the preheated oven for about 1 hour. You can use the knock test to find out whether the bread is done: Simply tap the bread with your knuckles: If it sounds hollow, the bread is done.
6. At the end of the baking time, take the bread out of the oven and let it cool down a

little. Then remove from the mold and let cool down completely.

16. Spicy party pizza bread

ingredients
- 1/4 l milk
- 1 pc egg (s)
- 500 g flour (smooth)
- 1 teaspoon of sugar
- 1 teaspoon salt
- 1 sachet of Knorr Basis (pasta asciutta)

- 30 g germ
- 100 g salami (whole)
- 100 g mountain cheese (whole)
- 1 onion (medium-sized)
- 1 pepper (large)
- 1 tbsp corn oil (Mazola) **preparation**

1. Put the milk, egg, flour, sugar, salt and Knorr base for pasta asciutta in a bowl and crumble the yeast over it. Knead the ingredients with the hand mixer until the dough separates from the edge of the bowl. Cut the salami and mountain cheese into 1/ 2 cm cubes. Peel the onion, cut into small pieces with the paprika and knead into the dough with the salami and mountain cheese. Let the dough rise for about 30 minutes. Shape a wake up, line a combi steamer tray with baking paper and place the party wake up on it.

For the oven:

2. Place the party wake on a Perfect Clean baking sheet and place in the oven preheated to 200 ° C, brush with water and bake for about 40 minutes.

17. Pumpkin seed bread

ingredients
- 800 g wheat flour
- 800 g rye flour
- 40 g fresh yeast (or 1 packet of dry yeast)
- 100 g Steirerkraft natural pumpkin seeds
- 1.5 l water (lukewarm)
- 2 teaspoons of salt **preparation**

1. For the pumpkin seed bread, briefly toast the natural pumpkin seeds in a pan without fat. Mix all ingredients together and knead with the lukewarm water to form a medium-firm dough. Let rise for 30 minutes at room temperature.
2. Preheat the oven to 220 ° C.
3. Knead the dough together and shape into a loaf or roll. Place on a baking sheet lined with baking paper and let rise again. The dough should rise by a third. Bake brown at 220 ° C for about 1 hour. Then let the pumpkin seed bread cool down on a wire rack.
4. The pumpkin seed bread tastes good with fresh nuts or simply spread thickly with butter or lard.

18. Sweet potato bread

ingredients
- 2 shallots
- 250 g sweet potatoes
- 1 tbsp vegetable oil
- 1/2 teaspoon fennel seeds
- 1/2 teaspoon coriander seeds
- 1/2 tsp ten
- 2 teaspoons of sea salt (coarse)
- 10 g yeast (fresh)
- 150 ml water (lukewarm)

- 100 g sourdough
- 200 g of wheat flour
- 150 g rye flour
- 150 g whole wheat flour **preparation**

1. For the sweet potato bread, first peel and finely chop the shallots. Peel and grate the sweet potato.
2. Heat some oil in a pan and fry the shallots in it without color. Add the grated sweet potato and fry briefly.
3. Toast the spices in a pan without fat until they smell fragrant. This releases the essential oils and the taste becomes more intense. Then grate finely in a mortar.
4. Dissolve the yeast in the water. Knead the sourdough, the sweet potatoes, the three types of flour and the spices with the dough hook of the mixer until a smooth dough is formed that loosens from the edge of the bowl. Remove and knead briefly by hand. Cover and let rise for about two hours.
5. Knead again and leave to rest covered for another quarter of an hour. In the meantime, line a baking sheet with parchment paper. Halve the bread dough and shape into loaves.

Place on the baking sheet with sufficient space, cover and let rise for another hour.
6. Shortly before the end of the walking time, preheat the oven to 220 ° C top / bottom heat. Score the top of the bread a few times and bake for a quarter of an hour. Then turn the temperature back to 180 ° C and bake the sweet potato bread for half an hour.

19. Spice bread

ingredients

- 500g flour
- 40 g of germ
- 125 ml milk (lukewarm)
- 1 pinch of sugar
- 2 onions (peeled, finely chopped)
- 1 clove of garlic (peeled, mashed)
- 50 g butter (liquid)
- 2 eggs
- 1 pinch of salt
- 1 pinch of nutmeg (grated)
- 1 teaspoon anise
- 1/2 teaspoon of fennel

- 2 tbsp dille (dried)
- 1 teaspoon rosemary (dried)
- Anise (for sprinkling) **preparation**

1. For the spicy bread, first sift the flour into a bowl, make a well and mix with the yeast, milk and sugar to form a thick dough. Cover and let rise for 15 minutes.
2. Knead with the remaining ingredients and cover and let rise for 30 minutes. Put the dough in a mold greased with butter, brush with water and sprinkle with aniseed.
3. Bake the seasoned bread in a preheated oven at 190 ° C for 40 minutes. Put a saucepan of water on the bottom of the oven.

20. Mixed bread

ingredients
- 500 g of wheat flour
- 500 g rye flour
- 1 teaspoon salt
- 750 ml of water
- 40 g of germ
- 1 teaspoon of fine granulated sugar

preparation
1. Prepare a dough for the mixed bread from the ingredients and let it rise in a warm place. Add a little more flour and knead again and let rise. Repeat this process two more times.

2. Bake in the preheated oven at 180–200 ° C for about 1–1 1/2 hours. Meanwhile, it is best to put a cup of water in the pipe. The bread is ready as soon as it sounds hollow when you knock on it.

GRILLED BREADS

21. Bread on a skewer

ingredients

- 500 g flour (smooth)
- 250 g milk (room temperature)
- 125 g butter (room temperature)
- 30 g germ
- 1/2 teaspoon salt
- 1 pinch of sugar
- olive oil
- Miscellaneous:
- thick wooden skewers

- possibly balancing act to tie

preparation

1. For the bread on a skewer, use half of the milk, the crumbled yeast and some flour to prepare a steamer. Dissolve the butter in the rest of the milk. As soon as the steam shows cracks, knead with the remaining dough ingredients to form a smooth dough. Cover the dough with a cloth and let rise in a warm place for 40 minutes.

2. Shape the dough into a roll . Cut off the slices and roll them into sticks with your hands. Wrap the dough sticks in a spiral around the wooden skewers, press the ends firmly or tie them with a splits. Let rise for another 15 minutes. Brush with olive oil and bake on the hot grill for about 10 minutes, until the bread on the skewer has turned a beautiful golden yellow color.

22. garlic bread

ingredients

- 1 baguette
- 8 cloves of garlic
- 1/2 bunch of parsley
- 8 tbsp olive oil

preparation

1. Slice the baguette diagonally.
2. Peel and finely chop the garlic cloves. Pluck the parsley leaves from the stems and also finely chop.
3. Mix the olive oil with the garlic and parsley in a bowl. Salt a little.

4. Place the baguette slices on a baking sheet and pour 1 teaspoon of garlic and parsley oil on each slice.
5. Grill the garlic bread in the preheated oven at 200 ° C until the bread is crispy.

23. Grilled toasted bread

ingredients
- 300 g roast leftovers
- 3 pieces of garlic cloves
- 1 piece of onion
- 1 tbsp parsley (chopped)
- 1 tbsp horseradish (grated)
- 250 g low-fat quark
- 1 egg yolk
- salt
- pepper
- 4 slices of black bread **preparation**

1. For the grilled toasted bread, cut the remaining roast, garlic and onion into small cubes.
2. Sauté the garlic and onion in a hot pan with a little oil, add the parsley and leftovers and fry for another 3 minutes.
3. Remove the roast mixture from the pan and let it cool down. Mix the roast mass with quark, horseradish and egg yolk in a bowl and season with salt and pepper.
4. Brush the black bread slices with the mixture and grill them indirectly at approx. 230 ° C for approx. 6-8 minutes, until the surface of the grilled toasted bread is golden brown.

24. Bread on a stick

ingredients

- 400 g whole wheat flour
- 300 ml milk (Lukewarm)
- 1 package dry yeast
- 1 tbsp honey
- 1 teaspoon salt
- 2 tbsp rosemary

preparation

1. For the bread on a stick, first mix dry germ and honey in the lukewarm milk and allow to swell for approx. 5 minutes (stir again and again).
2. In the meantime, weigh the flour and add salt. Then knead the flour, milk mixture and finely chopped, fresh rosemary with a mixer

or food processor and let rise in a warm environment for about 1 hour.
3. Prepare suitable stakes. For example, if you take sticks from bushes, peel them off at one end with a carving knife and clean them beforehand.
4. Roll the bread dough into individual long sausages and wrap them around the sticks in a spiral. Then hold them over the embers from the campire and turn them again and again until they are brownish and no longer soft.

25. Baked herb bread

ingredients

For the bread
- 1 cube of fresh yeast
- 300 g of flour
- 50 g durum wheat semolina
- 1 teaspoon of sugar
- 1 teaspoon salt
- 6 the olive oil
- Flour for the work surface
- Semolina for the work surface
- For the herb butter
- 2 handfuls of herbs B. basil, parsley, chervil
- 2 cloves of garlic
- 1 the olive oil
- 150 g soft butter

- salt
- pepper from the grinder
- 1 teaspoon of untreated lemon peel
- 1 of the lemon juice

Preparation steps

1. Mix the yeast with lukewarm water. Mix the flour with the semolina, sugar and salt in a bowl. Add the dissolved yeast with 4 tablespoons of olive oil and knead everything into a smooth dough using the dough hook of the electric hand mixer. Vary the amount of flour as required. Cover and let rise in a warm place for about 1 hour.
2. Knead the dough well again and form a long strand (approx. 50 cm) on a work surface sprinkled with flour and semolina. Place in a ring on a baking sheet lined with baking paper, press the ends together well. Cover with a cloth and let rest for another 30 minutes.
3. Preheat the oven to 200 ° C fan oven.

4. Brush the bread ring with the remaining oil and bake in the oven for about 40 minutes until golden brown.
5. Remove from the baking sheet and let cool down on a wire rack.
6. For the herb butter, rinse off the herbs, shake dry, pluck the leaves off and put them in a blender. Peel and add the garlic. Puree together with the oil. Stir the mixture into the softened butter and season with salt, pepper, lemon zest and lemon juice.
7. Cut into the bread every 2 cm, but do not cut all the way through. Place on baking paper and place aluminum foil underneath. Spread the herb butter into the incisions and bake the bread again in the oven for 10-15.
8. Take out, let cool down briefly and serve warm.

26. Filled white bread

ingredients

- 250 g wheat flour
- 2 tsp whole cane sugar
- 100 ml lukewarm milk (3.5% fat)
- 1 packet dry yeast
- 100 g jacket potato □ 2 tbsp liquid butter
- 200 g wheat flour type 1050
- 2 tsp salt
- 1 handful chives (10 g)
- 6 slices middle ages gouda

Preparation steps
1. Mix 100 g wheat flour with whole cane sugar, 100 ml lukewarm water, milk and yeast in a bowl and cover and let rise in a warm place for 30 minutes.
2. In the meantime, peel the potatoes and press them through a potato press. Knead the starter dough with the potatoes, butter, remaining flour, wheat flour type 1050 and salt. Shape into a ball and place on a baking sheet. Cover and let rise for about 1 hour, until the dough has doubled in volume.
3. Bake white bread in a preheated oven at 200 ° C for 30-40 minutes until golden brown. In the meantime, wash the chives, shake dry and cut into rolls. Cut the cheese into small pieces.
4. Let the bread cool down. Cut deeply into the shape of a lattice when it has cooled down. Fill the slices with chives and cheese, serve immediately.

27. Walnut bread

ingredients
- 500 g whole wheat flour
- 1 packet of dry yeast
- 10 g whole cane sugar (1 teaspoon)
- 2 sprigs of rosemary
- 150 g walnut kernels
- honey
- 1 teaspoon salt
- pepper
- 50 ml milk (1.5% fat)

- 50 ml of olive oil

Preparation steps
1. Mix the flour, yeast and sugar in a mixing bowl.
2. Stir in 250 ml of lukewarm water with the dough hook of the hand mixer until a uniform dough has formed. Cover and let rise in a warm place for about 30 minutes.
3. In the meantime, rinse off the rosemary, shake dry, pluck needles and chop.
4. Briefly toast the walnuts in a non-stick pan. Mix in the honey and rosemary and heat. Season with salt and pepper and place on a plate.
5. Heat the milk lukewarm, then stir into the dough with the oil. Knead in the nut-honey mixture until everything has bonded and the dough is shiny and smooth.
6. Shape the dough into a long loaf of bread and place on a baking sheet lined with baking paper. Cover and let rise in a warm place for about 20 minutes. Bake in the preheated oven at 220 ° C on the middle shelf for approx. 40 minutes.

28. Striploin steak with garlic bread

Ingredients

- 500 g striploin (here: from Scotch Beef & Scotch Lamb)
- Chimichurri
- ½ baguette
- olive oil, garlic, salt and pepper
- some fresh salad

Preparation
1. Take the steak out of the refrigerator about an hour before grilling so that it can reach room temperature. The fat cover is cut and the meat is rubbed on both sides with coarse sea salt.

Grilling
2. The grill is prepared for direct grilling at high heat and the steak is grilled using the well-known 90/90/90/90 method. For this purpose, the sizzle zone of the LE3 was used and the meat was then pulled in the grill at just under 150 ° C to a core temperature of approx. 54 ° C. In the meantime, the olive oil is mixed with a little salt, pepper and two pressed garlic cloves and spread on the cut baguette. The bread is now briefly grilled in the grill and then distributed on the salad. Add some chimichurri to it. The steak was very juicy and had a good taste. Salt and pepper support the sensational taste of the meat perfectly.

29. Low carb focaccia

ingredients
- 50 g sunflower seeds
- 50 g sesame
- 200 g almond flour
- 30 g linseed
- 5 eggs (size m)
- 200 g grained cream cheese
- 1 tbsp baking powder
- 1 tsp salt
- 4 tbsp olive oil
- 100 g black olives (pitted) ☐ 100 g

- tomatoes (fresh or dried)
- 2 tbsp italian herbs **Preparation steps**

1. Put the sunflower seeds together with the sesame seeds in a blender and process into fine flour. Then put in a bowl together with the almond flour and flaxseed.

2. Beat the eggs and mix with the whisk of a hand mixer. Mix the grainy cream cheese with a (stick) mixer to a smooth mass and add to the egg mixture together with baking powder, salt and olive oil. Mix everything together carefully.

3. Add the egg mixture to the flour mixture and stir in until an even low-carb focaccia batter is formed. Let rest in the bowl for around 5 minutes.

4. Place the dough on a baking sheet lined with baking paper or fill in a loaf pan. Press the typical dimples into the low-carb focaccia with your finger and bake for 15 minutes in a preheated oven at 180 ° C.

5. In the meantime, cut the olives and tomatoes in half as desired. If dried

tomatoes are used, cut them into large pieces.
6. Briefly take the low-carb focaccia out of the oven, cover with olives and tomatoes, carefully press and sprinkle with the Italian herbs. Bake until golden brown for another 5- 10 minutes. Let the finished low-carb focaccia cool down and serve with a little olive oil and salt.

30. Grill flatbread

ingredients

- 500g flour
- some salt (about 1/2 teaspoon)
- 2 tbsp spice (s) of your choice
- 1 pc. Dry yeast
- 250 ml of lukewarm water **preparation**

1. Mix all dry ingredients. Pour lukewarm water on top and mix with a dough hook to form a

smooth dough. Cover and let the dough rise for 60 minutes.

2. Then shape about 7 - 8 flatbreads and place on the grill. About 5 minutes on each side. Be careful not to burn. When the grill is very hot, set it aside. Or flip it over more often. Possibly break open 1 flatbread to see if the flatbread is ready.

3. Then serve hot. Tastes good, but also with garlic butter. If you want, you can add 1 clove of pressed garlic to the batter. Also delicious with fresh herbs such as rosemary or thyme.

31. Spicy grilled bread

ingredients

- 500g flour
- 350 ml of water
- 40 g yeast
- 1 toe / n garlic
- Onion (s) (fried onions)
- 200 g cheese, diced
- 200 g salami, diced
- 1 teaspoon of sugar
- 1 base (s) of salt

- Caraway seeds, whole or ground

- oregano

preparation

1. Mix the water, yeast and spices until the yeast has dissolved. Mix the flour, cheese and salami together and process with the liquid. Let the dough rest for 1 hour. Grease a springform pan and bake the bread at 180 ° C for about 45 minutes.

32. Herbal baguette

ingredients

- 1 baguette
- 1/2 bunch of basil
- 1/2 bunch of chives
- 1/2 bunch of parsley
- 1/2 bunch of oregano
- 1 teaspoon salt
- 100 g butter

preparation

1. For the herb baguette, first cut the herbs into small pieces. Mix the soft butter with the salt and the herbs.

2. Cut the baguette diagonally and spread the herb butter in the gaps.

3. Wrap the herb baguette in aluminum foil and grill on the grill for about 10 minutes.

33. Spicy bread on the grill

Ingredients

- 1 whole bread
- 100 gr butter
- 2 sprigs of fresh thyme
- 2 sprigs of fresh basil
- ¼ bunch of parsley
- Olive oil
- Salt

- Black pepper
- Red pepper

- 250 gr grated cheddar cheese

Preparation

1. Mix butter, finely chopped thyme, basil, parsley, salt and spices in a deep bowl. Slice the bread so that it does not break. Spread butter between each slice and sprinkle the cheddar cheese.

2. Spread the aluminum foil on the counter. Spread greaseproof paper and place the bread. Hover over a little olive oil. Gently wrap the paper around the edge. Roast for 15 minutes at overheated barbecue. Serve hot.

34. Suckling Pig Sandwich

Ingredients for

- suckling pig (pre-cooked),
- bread,
- lamb's lettuce,
- onions,
- cucumbers,
- tomatoes,
- BBQ sauce

Preparation

1. The frozen suckling pig is slowly thawed in the refrigerator the day before grilling. Lamb's lettuce, cucumber and tomatoes are washed and prepared for the sandwich topping. The onion is cut into rings.

Grilling

1. The grill (or oven) is first heated to 120 ° C indirect heat. The meat is placed on a fireproof dish filled with water with an insert so that the fat drips into the water. The meat is fried in this way for about 60 minutes. To give the crust the perfect finish, the temperature is increased to approx. 200 ° C after 60 minutes. It is now important that you get enough top heat for the crust. If necessary, you can also place the meat with the crust down directly over the heat. After about 15 minutes the crust should be ready. But here please act according to your feelings so that the crust does not burn - that would be a shame! The

bread slices are briefly toasted on both sides over direct heat.

35. Crispy bread and cheese salad

ingredients
- 120 g wholemeal rye bread (3 slices)
- 30 g sultanas
- 4 tbsp fruit vinegar
- salt
- pepper
- 4 tbsp safflower oil
- 300 g apples (e.g., elstar, 2 apples)
- 1 ½ bunch radish

- 100 g sliced cheese (e.g., leerdammer, 17% absolute fat)
- 1 bunch flat leaf parsley

Preparation steps

1. Cut the bread into 1 cm cubes and roast them in a non-oiled pan over medium heat for about 4 minutes until crispy. Put on a plate and let cool down.

2. In the meantime, rinse the sultanas with hot water and drain. Mix fruit vinegar with a little salt, pepper and safflower oil to make a salad dressing.

3. Wash the apples, cut each apple from 4 sides towards the center into approximately 5 mm thick slices, cut the slices into cubes. Mix the apple cubes and sultanas with the dressing.

4. Wash, drain and clean the radishes. Put small radish leaves aside; Quarter the radishes.

5. Cut the cheese slices into 2 cm squares. Wash the parsley, shake dry and pluck the leaves.

6. Mix the cheese, parsley and radish leaves, radishes and apple dressing. Season to taste with salt and pepper.

7. Put the lettuce in a well-closing, large food storage container (approx. 1.5 l content) to transport. Put the bread cubes in a smaller food storage container (approx. 500 m capacity) and sprinkle over the cheese and radish salad before serving.

36. Turkey cream cheese rolls

Ingredients
- 4 slices of turkey breast
- 5 g poultry seasoning mix
- 15 black olives
- 4 sun-dried tomatoes
- 150 g cream cheese
- 1 tbsp breadcrumbs
- 1 tbsp Herbs of Provence

Preparation
1. For this recipe we need slices of turkey breast that are as thin as possible. To do this, the turkey breast slices are worked again with a beater, similar to the one known from the schnitzel, until they are evenly thin.
2. The thinly pounded meat is sprinkled with the poultry spice mixture. Then it comes to the filling, cut the tomatoes and olives into small pieces and mix them with the cream cheese. To improve the consistency of this mass, breadcrumbs are added.
3. Brush the turkey slices with the cheese mixture and sprinkle with herbs from Provence. The finished slice of meat must now be rolled up. It is important that the meat slice is rolled up tightly, otherwise it could fall apart on the grill.
4. So that our turkey breast roll can shine not only in terms of taste, but also aesthetically on the grill, we make a roll skewer out of the roll. Cut the roll into pieces approx. 3 cm wide and skewer 3-4 pieces flat.

37. Cevapcici in flatbread

Ingredients

- 1 kg minced meat (mixed beef/lamb or beef/pork)
- 1 large onion
- 3 cloves of garlic a
- little fresh parsley
- 1 tbsp olive oil
- 1 tbsp salt
- 3 tsp paprika powder
- 3 tsp pepper, finely ground
- Flatbread

- salad □ ajvar
- hot peppers

Preparation
1. The onion is finely grated (not chopped), the garlic cloves are pressed, the parsley finely chopped. The minced meat is mixed well with onion, garlic, parsley and the other ingredients so that the spices are evenly distributed.
2. Now you form thumb-thick cevapcici, about 7 cm long. The use of the Cevapomaker is suitable here, with which you can form seven Cevapcici in one course. *Grilling*
   1. The grill is prepared for direct grilling over medium heat. The cevapcici are placed on the hot grid, turned after 3 - 4 minutes and grilled on the other side. Then the cevapcici is removed from the grill and we prepare the flatbreads. The flatbread is topped with salad and 6 - 7 cevapcici are placed on top. Spread 2 - 3 tablespoons of ajar over it and place two peppers on top.

38. Breads with smoked salmon

ingredients

For the spread
- 100 g cream cheese
- 1 ½ tbsp horseradish from the jar
- 1 pinch grained vegetable broth
- 1 pinch paprika powder
- 50 g whipped cream beaten
- salt
- pepper
- 4 slice whole grain bread
- 4 larger slices of smoked salmon

- 1 red chilli pepper
- 2 tbsp sunflower seeds
- 1 tbsp chopped parsley

Preparation steps

1. Mix the cream cheese with the horseradish, the stock and the paprika until smooth. Fold in the cream and season with salt and pepper.
2. Spread the spread on the bread and top with salmon. Wash the chillies, remove the seeds, cut into rings, and mix with the sunflower seeds and parsley. Garnish the bread with it and serve immediately.

39. Gratinated bread

ingredients

- 3 pc. Cocktail tomatoes
- 8 pcs. Capers (from the jar)
- 70 g mozzarella
- 1 pc. Pita bread
- 80 g brunch paprika peppers
- 4 slice (s) of Parma ham
- Pepper (freshly ground)

preparation

1. Wash tomatoes. Cut tomatoes, capers and mozzarella into slices.
2. Spread brunch on bread. Cover one after the other with tomatoes, capers and mozzarella.

Gratinate for approx. 5 minutes under the hot grill of the oven. Top with ham and sprinkle with pepper.

40. Small Flatbreads

ingredients

- 500 g whole wheat flour
- 21 g fresh yeast (0.5 cubes)
- 1 tsp honey
- 1 tsp salt
- 70 ml olive oil
- 7 spring onions

Preparation steps

1. Sift the flour into a large bowl, making a well in the middle. Crumble the yeast in the well, pour honey and 4 tablespoons of lukewarm water over it. Dust with a little flour from the edge and cover the pre-dough in a warm and draft-free place for about 10 minutes.

2. Add salt, 4 tablespoons of olive oil and about 200 ml of lukewarm water to the pre-dough and use the dough hook of a hand mixer to form a smooth dough. Cover with a damp tea towel and let rise at room temperature for about 1 hour.

3. In the meantime, wash and clean the spring onions and cut into fine rolls.

4. Knead the dough well again on a floured work surface with the spring onion rolls and approximately 2 tablespoons of olive oil. Then divide into 8 pieces. Roll out into small flatbreads with a rolling pin and brush with the rest of the oil. Grill on the hot grill on

both sides for approx. 10-15 minutes while turning.

BREAD FOR BREAKFAST

41. Fitness bread

ingredients

- 300 g wholemeal rye flour
- 300 g whole wheat flour
- 2 teaspoons of salt
- 2 tbsp honey
- 50 g germ

- 2 tbsp rapeseed beer
- 70 g pumpkin seeds
- 75 g walnut kernels
- 100 g apricots (dried)
- Milk for brushing **preparation**

1. Mix both types of flour and salt. Mix honey and yeast with 1/2 liter of lukewarm water. Add to the flour together with the oil. Knead vigorously for up to 10 minutes.

2. Cover and let rise in a warm place for about 25 minutes. Roughly chop the pumpkin, walnuts and apricots, add to the dough and knead again. Shape a loaf or put the dough in a coated loaf pan. Brush with milk and cover again for 15 minutes.

3. Place a bowl with cold water in the pipe and bake bread at 180 ° C for about 60 minutes (do not preheat)

42. Cocoa and Orange Bread

ingredients

- 250 ml milk (1.5% fat)
- 1 cube of yeast (fresh)
- 3 tbsp orange blossom honey
- 1 orange (organic)
- 300 g spelled flour
- 80 g corn grits
- 100 g almonds (ground, roasted)
- 10 g of salt

- 50 g cocoa powder
- Flour (for working) **preparation**

1. For cocoa and orange bread, warm the milk to lukewarm. Crumble the yeast in half of the milk. Dissolve these with the honey in the milk and let stand until bubbles appear.

2. Wash the orange with hot water, rub dry, finely grate the peel and fillet the orange, collecting the juice. Cut the fillets into small pieces. Add 2 tbsp of the orange juice to the rest of the milk.

3. Put the spelled flour, corn grits, almonds, salt, cocoa powder, orange peel and fillets in a mixing bowl. Finally, pour in the yeast-milk mixture. While kneading with the dough hook on a low setting with the food processor, gradually add enough of the remaining milk until an airy, homogeneous dough is formed.

4. Knead the dough on the floured work surface for about 5 minutes with the balls of your hands, repeatedly beating it up and turning it

until it is no longer sticky and elastic, then cover it in a bowl for about 2 hours until its volume has doubled.

5. Cover a baking sheet with parchment paper, place the dough on it as a ball with the dough top facing down, and cut crosswise. Cover and let the dough rest for about 1 hour until the volume has doubled.

6. Preheat the oven to 220 °C (convection not suitable). Brush the surface of the bread with water and bake the bread on the second rack from the bottom for 40-45 minutes. Take the finished cocoa and orange bread out of the oven and let it cool down completely on a wire rack.

43. Whole meal spelled bread

ingredients

- 500 g whole meal spelled flour
- 15 g of salt
- 7 g dry yeast
- 5 g bread spice
- 70 g sesame seeds
- 70 g sunflower seeds

- 70 g pumpkin seeds

- 15 g caraway seeds (whole)
- 500 ml water (lukewarm)

- Seeds (for sprinkling)

preparation

1. Mix all dry ingredients, knead with water and cover and leave for 30 minutes.

2. Line the loaf pan with baking paper and add the dough.

3. Sprinkle with seeds and bake the bread in the preheated oven at 190 ° C for about 75 minutes. Place a saucepan with water on the bottom of the oven.

44. Herb egg bread with tomato cream

ingredients

- 2 slice (s) of black bread
- 1 spring onion (small, washed, cut into rings)
- Cress (for sprinkling)
- 2 tbsp butter (for frying)

For the tomato cream:

- 4 tbsp cream cheese
- 6 tbsp tomato paste

- salt

- Pepper (from the mill)

For the herb egg dish:

- 4 eggs

- 1 shot of mineral water

- 1/2 bunch of parsley (washed, finely chopped) ☐ 1/2 bunch of chives (washed, cut into rolls)

- 1 handful of sprouts (of your choice, e.g. red cabbage sprouts)

- salt

- Pepper (from the mill)

- 1 pinch nutmeg (grated) **preparation**

1. For herb egg bread, beat the eggs with tomato cream, sprinkle with mineral water and season well with salt, pepper and nutmeg. Stir in herbs.
2. Melt the butter in a pan. As soon as the butter starts to bubble, pour the herb-egg mixture into the pan and let it set slowly, stirring again and again. As soon as the egg dish is firm at the bottom but still slightly runny at the top, remove the pan from the heat and set aside.
3. For the tomato cream, roughly mix the cream cheese with 2 tablespoons of tomato paste, season with salt & pepper. Halve the bread slices to taste and brush with 2 tablespoons of tomato paste each, then spread the tomato cream on top. "Pick up" herb egg dishes with a fork and spread on the bread.
4. Sprinkle herb egg bread with tomato cream with cress and spring onion and serve.

45. Kamut bread with oats and millet

ingredients *For 2 loaves of bread:*
- 30 g of salt
- 40 g yeast
- 600 ml of water
- 50 g sourdough
- 850 g wholegrain kamut flour (finely ground)
- 150 g whole oat flour (medium coarsely ground)
- 100 g millet (freshly ground)
- Bread spices (anise, fennel, caraway, coriander - to taste)

preparation
1. For the kamut bread, dissolve the salt and yeast in water, process with the sourdough and the remaining ingredients to form a rather soft dough.
2. Let rest for 45 minutes.
3. Divide into 2 equal pieces, round out and then shape into wigs.
4. Roll in oatmeal or oat bran, place in bread baking tins.
5. Let rest again for 45 minutes.
6. Preheat the oven to 250 ° C, place a vessel with water on top.
7. Add the bread and turn back to 180 ° C after 3 minutes.
8. The Kamutbrot let cool before slicing good.

46. Fitness bread with smoked trout

ingredients

- 1 apple
- 2 pieces of avocado
- 1 tbsp lemon juice
- 4 tbsp crème fraîche
- 2 teaspoons of horseradish
- Salt pepper
- 4 whole grain bread (large slices)
- 150 g trout fillets (smoked)

- 4 tbsp beetroot sprouts **preparation**

1. For the fitness bread with smoked trout, wash the apple, quarter, core and cut into narrow strips.

2. Halve the avocado, stone, peel and cut into strips.

3. Drizzle the apple and avocado strips with lemon juice.

4. Mix the crème fraîche with the horseradish, season with salt and pepper.

5. Spread 1 tablespoon of horseradish cream on each slice of bread.

6. Place the avocado and apple strips on top, season with salt and pepper.

7. Pluck the trout fillets into bite-sized pieces and distribute them on the bread.

8. Garnish with the beetroot sprouts.

47. Fried egg in crispy bread

ingredients

- 2 slices of a sandwich roll (thick)
- 4 slices of bacon
- 2 pc eggs

preparation

1. Preheat the oven to grill setting.
2. Cut slices about 3 cm thick from the bread or brioche. Cut out a hole with a diameter of approx. 5 cm.

3. Sear 2 overlapping slices of breakfast bacon in a pan. Place bread slices on top and fry them.

4. Beat an egg in each of the holes and season to taste. Cover and fry over a medium heat for 5-7 minutes, until the eggs start to thicken.

5. Now slide the pan without the lid onto the top rail in the oven until the bread is toasted until it is golden brown and the eggs are whole.

6. Remove, arrange on plates with the garnish and serve sprinkled with chives.

48. Tramezzini with tuna

ingredients

- 12 slice (s) of tramezzini bread (soft, juicy white bread without crust)
- 200 g tuna (white meat, marinated in oil)
- 1 tbsp lemon juice
- 4 tbsp mayonnaise
- 1 tbsp cognac
- Sea salt (from the mill)
- Pepper (from the mill)

preparation

1. Puree the tuna with the lemon juice.

2. Mix with the mayonnaise, season with salt, pepper and cognac.

3. Spread it thickly over half of the bread and cover with the second half.

4. Cut each bread diagonally into two triangles.

49. Olive bread

ingredients

- 500g flour
- 1 package dry yeast
- 2 teaspoons of salt
- 300 ml water (lukewarm)
- 100 g Kalamata olives (in oil or brine)
- Oregano (dried)

- pepper
- 2 tbsp olive oil

preparation

1. Knead a medium-strength yeast dough from flour, dry yeast, salt and lukewarm water and cover in a warm place.

2. Halve and core the olives.

3. Roll out the dough into two slices, one slightly larger than the other. Place the larger slice on the greased and floured tray. Spread the olives on top and season with oregano and pepper.

4. Place the second sheet of pastry on top, press the edges together well and brush the flatbread with olive oil. Prick the surface several times with a fork, let rise for 30 minutes.

5. Put in a preheated oven at 180 ° C and bake for about 30 minutes.

50. Brightened banana bread

Ingredients

- 1 pack of low-fat cream cheese (227 grams)
- A cup with a capacity of
- 130 ml containing butter
- A 3/8-liter bowl containing sugar
- 2 eggs
- A bowl with a capacity of
- 3/8 liter with ripe bananas, pureed
- 1/2 teaspoon vanilla extract
- A bowl with a capacity of
- 3/4 liter containing all-purpose flour
- 1/2 teaspoon baking soda
- 1/2 teaspoon baking soda

- 1/2 teaspoon salt
- A bowl with a capacity of
- 1/4 liter with pecans, chopped and split

Preparation

1. In a large bowl mix the cream cheese, the butter and the sugar well.
2. Add eggs one after the other, which hit well after each addition.
3. Stir in bananas and vanilla.
4. Mix flour, baking powder, baking powder and salt. Gradually add to the cream mixture until it is moistened.
5. Fold in 130 liters of pecans.
6. Place on 2 cm x 1 cm loaf pans coated with non-stick cooking spray.
7. Sprinkle with the remaining pecans.
8. Bake at 170 degrees for 55-60 minutes or until a toothpick comes out clean near the center.

51. Microwave bread

Ingredients
- 3 tbsp wheat fiber
- 2 tbsp of natural yogurt
- 1 tablespoon baking powder (cake) ☐ Oil for greasing ☐ Salt to taste.
- 3 tablespoons fine oatmeal
- 1 egg

Method of Preparation
1. Add in a bowl the egg and plain yogurt and mix.
2. Add the wheat fiber, oats and mix.
3. Add the baking powder and salt and mix until smooth.

4. Grease a microwave-safe square pot with olive oil, add the batter and arrange to stand straight and microwave for 2 minutes.

52. Creamy Cucumber Sandwiches

Ingredients
- 85 g cream cheese
- 1 medium cucumber
- 1 tbsp sour cream
- 1/8 tsp salt
- 1 pinch of pepper
- 1/8 tsp garlic powder
- Almond flour bread or other low-carb bread

Preparation
1. Grate the cucumber and let the excess liquid drain.

2. Mix cream cheese, cucumber, and sour cream until smooth. Season with salt, pepper and garlic powder.
3. Cut the slices of low-carb bread in half to make them thinner. Put the cucumber mixture on the bottom slice and cover it with the top slice. Cut in half.

53. Fluffy Protein Bread With Nutri-Plus

Ingredients
- 90 g neutral Nutri-Plus protein powder
- 200 g Cashews
- 200 g linseed
- 500 g Unsweetened soya yogurt
- 150 ml of   water
- 100 g Sunflower seeds
- 1 pck. baking powder
- 1/2 tsp salt

Preparation
1. First put the cashews, linseed and protein powder in a blender and chop everything together to a coarse flour.
2. Then pour the soy yogurt, water, baking soda and salt into a bowl and add the cashew protein powder mixture.
3. Third Stir everything into a smooth dough and fill it into a baking paper-lined form.
4. Let the dough shell for about 10-15 minutes. In time, you can preheat the oven to 175 ° C.
5. Bake the bread for about 60 minutes. To make sure it's really baked through, do the stick test.
6. Allow cooling, to taste delicious and then let taste.

54. Microwave Quick Keto Bread

Ingredients
- 3 tbsp. almond flour
- ½ tsp psyllium powder
- ½ tsp baking powder
- A pinch of salt
- 1 large egg

Preparation
1. Add the dry ingredients to a small bowl, then butter and egg. Mix well.
2. Lubricate the microwave, mug, or small bowl, and add the batter.
3. Put the bread in the microwave for 80-100 seconds.
4. Gently place the bread on a cutting board and cut in half.

55. Cheese bread with bacon

Ingredients
- 200 g bacon
- 1/2 cup almond flour
- 1 tbsp baking powder
- 1/3 cup sour cream
- large eggs
- tbsp melted butter
- 1 cup grated cheddar cheese

Preparation
1. Preheat the oven to 148 degrees. Oil the baking tray. Then cut the bacon into cubes and fry it in a pan until crisp.
2. Beat almond flour and baking powder.
3. Beat sour cream and eggs.
4. Mix wet and dry ingredients together.
5. Add the butter and mix, then add the bacon and cheddar cheese.
6. Put the dough in a bread pan. Garnish the top with a little cheese.
7. Bake for 45 minutes, then insert a wooden toothpick into the center. The bread will be ready when the toothpick comes out clean.
8. Let the bread cool before slicing, because if you cut it hot, it may fall apart. Better yet, if you keep the bread in the refrigerator before serving.

56. Cheese Halibut Cheese Bread

Ingredient

- 450-900 g halibut (about 6 fillets)
- 1 slice of butter
- 3 tbsp grated parmesan
- 1 tbsp bread crumbs
- 1 tsp salt
- ½ tsp black pepper
- 2 tsp garlic powder
- 1 tbsp dried parsley

Preparation
1. Preheat the oven to 204 degrees. Thoroughly mix all the ingredients in a bowl except platus.
2. Dry the fish fillet with a paper towel and place each part on a baking sheet with parchment, oiled.
3. Lay the cheese mixture into pieces of fish so that it covers its upper part.
4. Bake the fish for 10-12 minutes (turn the pan at least once).
5. Increase the heat by 2-3 minutes until the top is golden brown. Check for readiness with a fork.

57. Grilled Eggplant Sandwich

Ingredient
- 1 medium eggplant (or 2 small zucchini)
- 1 to 2 tablespoons low-sodium soy sauce (use wheat-free soy sauce if you are gluten sensitive)
- 1 tablespoon balsamic vinegar
- 8 large, thick slices of whole-grain bread or gluten-free bread
- 1 roasted red pepper, sliced

- 1 large roasted garlic head
- 4 teaspoons of Dijon mustard (optional)
- 4 leaves of red lettuce **Preparation**
1. Cut the eggplant diagonally into slices 1/4 inch (6 mm).
2. Brush the eggplant slices with soy sauce and roast them on a grill or iron skillet seasoned over medium-high heat for 2 to 4 minutes on each side until they are soft and lightly browned.
3. Remove them from the pan and sprinkle with vinegar. Set them aside. Toast the bread, if desired and spread 2 to 4 cloves of garlic in the lower slice, add a layer of grilled eggplant, folding the soft pieces to fit in the slice of bread.
4. Top with slices of roasted red pepper and lettuce. Spread mustard over the top slice of bread, if desired, then complete the sandwich and serve.

58. Cucumber and kale open sandwich

Ingredient
- 2 slices of whole-grain bread, toasted
- 2 to 3 tablespoons of hummus prepared without tahini or oil
- 1 chopped green onion
- $\frac{1}{4}$ cup chopped fresh cilantro
- 2 medium kale leaves, chopped into small bitesized pieces (about the size of coriander leaves)
- $\frac{1}{2}$ small cucumber
- Mustard of your choice

- Lemon pepper (Mrs. Dash and Frontier brands have no salt)

Preparation
1. Spread hummus generously on toasted bread. Sprinkle the green onion, cilantro, and kale evenly over the hummus.
2. Slice the cucumber in 8 circles and spread each with a thin layer of mustard.
3. Place the cucumber slices, with the mustard down, on top of the coriander and kale layer and press down, if necessary, so that they remain in place.
4. Sprinkle the open sandwich generously with lemon pepper, cut it in half or quarters, if desired, and serve.

59. Spinach Cheese Bread

Ingredients

- 225 g almond flour
- 2 tsp baking powder
- ½ tsp salt
- 100 g soft butter
- 85 g fresh spinach, chopped
- 1 clove garlic, finely chopped
- 1 tbsp chopped rosemary
- 2 large eggs

- 140 g grated cheddar cheese

Preparation
1. Preheat the oven to 200 degrees.
2. Put the almond flour, baking powder and salt in a large bowl. Mix well, then add oil and mix again.
3. Add the remaining ingredients (if you wish, you can leave a little cheddar for the top of the bread). Mix well.
4. Put the dough in a cast-iron skillet, greased with oil, and form a pancake with a thickness of about 3.5-4 cm.
5. Bake for 25-30 minutes; then leave the bread in the pan for 15 minutes to cool.

60. Tramezzini with ham and gorgonzola

ingredients

- 2 slice (s) of tramezzini bread (soft white bread without crust)
- 80-100 g ham (sliced ham)
- 50 g cheese (Gorgonzola)
- 1 pc. Tomato (s)

- some pepper (ground) **preparation**

1. Top half of the ham on a tramezzini bread. Cut the tomato into slices and place on top. Grate the Gorgonzola directly onto it with a coarse grater and distribute it evenly. Season with crushed pepper. Top with the rest of the ham and cover with the second slice of bread. Cut diagonally into two triangles with a sharp knife. Serve immediately or store in a cool place wrapped in cling film so that the juicy white bread does not dry out.

SNACKS

61. Gratinated bread

ingredients
- 3 pc. Cocktail tomatoes
- 8 pcs. Capers (from the jar)
- 70 g mozzarella
- 1 pc. Pita bread
- 80 g brunch paprika hot peppers
- 4 slice (s) of Parma ham

- Pepper (freshly ground)

preparation
1. Wash tomatoes. Cut the tomatoes, capers and mozzarella into slices.
2. Spread brunch on bread. Top one after the other with tomatoes, capers and mozzarella. Gratinate for approx. 5 minutes under the hot grill of the oven. Top with ham and sprinkle with pepper.

62. Bread cheese skewers

ingredients

- 2 slice (s) of pumpernickel
- 25 g skimmed cream cheese
- 50 g whole, low-fat semi-hard cheese
- 1/4 cucumber
- 1/4 apple
- 4 pieces of cocktail tomatoes
- Salt pepper
- 2 wooden skewers **preparation**

1. For the bread and cheese skewers, halve the pumpernickel slices, coat halved pumpernickel slices with 1 tablespoon of cream cheese, place another slice of bread on top, coat with cream cheese again, put third slice on top, coat with cream cheese and finish with pumpernickel.
2. Cut the bread block into 2 cm cubes. Also cut the semi-hard cheese into slightly smaller cubes. Cut the apple into three wedges.
3. Put alternately pumpernickel blocks, cucumber slices, apple pieces, cheese cubes and tomatoes on the wooden skewers. Then sprinkle the bread cheese skewers with a little salt and plenty of freshly ground pepper.

63. Herbal bread terrine with currant

ingredients

- 500 g saucepan
- 175 g cream cheese
- 50 g herbs (mixed - oregano, thyme, basil,)
- salt
- pepper
- 4 sheets of gelatin
- 200 g prosciutto
- 100 ml whipped cream
- 200 g currants (red and yellow)

- 20 slice (s) of bread **preparation**
1. For the herb and bread terrine, wash the currants, drain them well and peel them off the stems. Debark the bread slices. For the terrine cream, wash the herbs, shake dry and chop finely.
2. Cream cheese, curd cheese, the herbs and spices mix well.
3. Soak the gelatine in cold water. In the meantime, heat the whipped cream a little (do not boil!) And dissolve the squeezed gelatine in it. Then quickly stir into the cream cheese curd mixture.
4. Finally mix in the currants.
5. For the herb and bread terrine, line a loaf pan with cling film.
6. Line a loaf pan with cling film. The bottom layer is filled with the bread crusts, then spread on the cream, put on the prosciutto and finish with the bread slices. Repeat this sequence a few times.
7. Let the terrine cool for a few hours.
8. Some time before serving, take the herb and bread terrine with currant out of the refrigerator, turn it out of the mold and decorate with currant and fresh herbs.

64. Kamut bread with oats and millet

ingredients *For 2 loaves of bread:*
- 30 g of salt
- 40 g yeast
- 600 ml of water
- 50 g sourdough
- 850 g wholegrain kamut flour (finely ground)
- 150 g whole oat flour (medium coarsely ground)
- 100 g millet (freshly ground)

- Bread spices (anise, fennel, caraway, coriander - to taste)

preparation
1. For the kamut bread, dissolve the salt and yeast in water, process with the sourdough and the remaining ingredients to form a rather soft dough.
2. Let rest for 45 minutes.
3. Divide into 2 equal pieces, round out and then shape into wigs.
4. Roll in oatmeal or oat bran, place in bread baking tins.
5. Let rest again for 45 minutes.
6. Preheat the oven to 250 ° C, place a vessel with water on top.
7. Add the bread and turn back to 180 ° C after 3 minutes.
8. The Kamutbrot let cool before slicing good.

65. Ham sandwich

ingredients

- 4 slice (s) of light sourdough bread
- 2 tbsp olive oil
- 120 g rocket
- 200 g goat cream cheese
- 200 g ham (thinly sliced)

For the pepper jam:

- 2 peppers (red)
- 2 tomatoes (medium-sized)
- 2 clove (s) of garlic
- 1 shallot
- 2 tbsp apple cider vinegar
- 3 tbsp sugar (brown)
- 2 tbsp lemon juice (fresh)
- salt
- Pepper (black)
- Cayenne pepper **preparation**

1. Halve the tomatoes, place a coarse grater on an empty bowl, rub the tomatoes on top, discard the bowl.

2. Put the tomatoes in a pan, turn to medium heat. Finely chop the bell pepper, peel the shallot and garlic cloves, chop finely. Add the peppers, shallots, garlic and the remaining ingredients to the pan, bring to the boil, reduce the heat so that the jam simmered

gently. Let simmer for 45 minutes, or until syrupy.
3. Let cool and pour into a jam jar. Goes well with sandwiches, but also with grilled and Asian dishes.

4. Keeps closed in the refrigerator

66. Bruschette with egg topping

ingredients

- 2 pc eggs (hard-boiled)
- 2 tbsp pickles (chopped)
- 2 tbsp cucumber (chopped)
- 2 tbsp sour cream
- salt
- pepper
- 1 tbsp parsley (finely chopped)

preparation

1. For the bruschette with egg topping, mix all the ingredients well and season. Brown the bread slices in the oven preheated to 250 ° C for about 4 minutes. Brush with the egg topping and serve immediately.

67. Tramezzini with tuna

ingredients

- 12 slice (s) of tramezzini bread (soft, juicy white bread without crust)

- 200 g tuna (white meat, marinated in oil)

- 1 tbsp lemon juice

- 4 tbsp mayonnaise

- 1 tbsp cognac
- Sea salt (from the mill)

- Pepper (from the mill) **preparation**

1. Puree the tuna with the lemon juice.

2. Mix with the mayonnaise, season with salt, pepper and cognac.

3. Spread it thickly over half of the bread and cover with the second half.

4. Cut each bread diagonally into two triangles.

68. potato bread

ingredients

- 1/2 cube of germ
- 1 cup of water (lukewarm)
- 250 g of flour
- 250 g potato flakes (coarse)
- 1 tbsp salt
- 2 tbsp olive oil (and a little olive oil to grease the tray)

- 375 ml of water

preparation

1. For the potato bread, crumble the yeast in a saucepan and mix with the lukewarm water. Let rest for about 5 minutes.

2. Then mix the flour, the potato flakes, salt, 1 tablespoon of olive oil and the water into the mixed yeast and slowly knead everything in the food processor for 5 minutes - the ingredients should combine well and form a smooth dough.

3. Put the dough back in the pan, dust with a little flour and cover with a cloth. Let rise for at least an hour.

4. Then brush a baking sheet with olive oil and line with baking paper. Place the dough in the middle of the baking sheet, drizzle with the remaining olive oil and use your fingertips to spread the dough evenly on the baking sheet from the inside out.

5. The dough should be about 1 cm high and have small dents on the surface due to the pressure of the fingertips - like an Italian

focaccia. Let the dough rise for another half an hour on the baking sheet.

6. In the meantime, preheat the oven to 250 degrees. Bake the bread in the hot oven for 30 minutes. Then immediately remove from the baking sheet, turn over and allow to evaporate.

69. Avocado bread

ingredients

- 1 avocado (ripe)
- 2 slice (s) of bread
- 100 g cheese (of your choice)
- Spices (e.g. salt, pepper, chilli)

preparation

1. For the avocado bread, first peel the avocado and remove the stone. Mash half an avocado onto a slice of bread with a fork. Season with spices of your choice (chilli flakes, salt and pepper or roast chicken spices are particularly delicious).

2. Put the cheese on top (soft cheese in slices, harder ones should be grated beforehand) and let it melt in the oven at 180-200 ° C for 5 minutes, preferably with the grill function. It is essential to keep an eye on so that the cheese does not burn on the avocado bread.

70. Olive bread

ingredients

- 500g flour
- 1 package dry yeast
- 2 teaspoons of salt
- 300 ml water (lukewarm)
- 100 g Kalamata olives (in oil or brine)
- Oregano (dried)
- pepper

- 2 tbsp olive oil

preparation

1. Knead a medium-strength yeast dough from flour, dry yeast, salt and lukewarm water and cover in a warm place.

2. Halve and core the olives.

3. Roll out the dough into two slices, one slightly larger than the other. Place the larger slice on the greased and floured tray. Spread the olives on top and season with oregano and pepper.

4. Place the second sheet of pastry on top, press the edges together well and brush the flatbread with olive oil. Prick the surface several times with a fork, let rise for 30 minutes.

5. Put in a preheated oven at 180 ° C and bake for about 30 minutes.

71. Eggplant cream on spelled buckwheat bread

ingredients

- 2 aubergines
- 2 cloves of garlic
- 100 ml of olive oil
- 1 lemon (juice and zest)
- 1/2 teaspoon cumin (ground)
- sea-salt

- Pepper (from the mill)
- 1 teaspoon sesame (toasted)
- 6 slice (s) of spelled buckwheat bread
- 2 stalk (s) spring onions (cut into rings)
- Coriander (plucked) **preparation**

1. Preheat the oven to 180 ° C. Line a baking sheet with parchment paper.

2. Halve the aubergine lengthways and cut into the flesh in a diamond shape, taking care not to damage the skin.

3. Peel and finely chop the garlic. Press between the diamonds in the aubergine pulp.

4. Place the aubergines on the baking sheet, pour olive oil over them and season with salt. Put in the oven for 45-50 minutes.

5. Scrape out the pulp and place in a tall mug. Add lemon zest, lemon juice, cumin, salt and

pepper and puree finely. Stir in the sesame seeds.

6. Fry the bread slices in a pan with a little olive oil until crispy.

7. Spread the eggplant cream on top. Sprinkle with spring onions and coriander leaves.

72. Crispy fish bread

ingredients

- 1 focaccia
- 250 g fish fillet (white, skinless, preferably cod)
- salt
- pepper
- 3 tbsp flour
- 1 egg
- 8 tbsp panko flour (or finely grated white bread (Mie de Pain))

- Vegetable oil (for deep-frying; amount depending on the size of the pan or deep fryer)
- 1 tuber (s) beetroot (pre-cooked)
- 2 tbsp mayonnaise
- 1 squirt of lemon juice
- 1 handful of garden cress **preparation**

1. For the crispy fish bread, cut the fish fillets into small rectangles and season with salt & pepper. For a crispy breading, first turn the fish pieces in flour, then pull them through the beaten egg and finally turn them in panko flour or mie de pain.

2. In a deep pan or in the deep fryer, fry the breaded fish at approx. 160 ° C, swimming in oil, until golden brown. Drain the fish on kitchen paper.

3. In the meantime, quarter the focaccia and cut in half horizontally. Cover the undersides of the bread with thinly sliced beetroot slices.

4. Refine the mayonnaise with a little lemon juice and spread on the beetroot. Place a crispy piece of fish on top and garnish the

crispy fish bread with garden cress. Depending on your taste, the top of the focaccia can be used as a "lid".

73. Onion bread with goat cheese

ingredients

- 4 onions (red, approx. 300 g)
- 1 tbsp butter
- 2 teaspoons of sugar
- 1/2 teaspoon chilli flakes
- 100 ml red wine (dry or red grape juice)
- salt

- 4 slice (s) of farmer's bread (large)
- 150 g goat camembert **preparation**

1. For the onion bread with goat cheese, peel the onions, quarter them and cut into fine strips. Melt the butter with the sugar in a pan. Stir in the onions with the chilli flakes and fry over a medium to low heat for about 5 minutes. Pour in red wine or grape juice and cook for about 13 minutes until the liquid is creamy, then season with salt.

2. Preheat the oven to 250 degrees (switch on now: convection 230 degrees). Cover the baking sheet with parchment paper.

3. Place the bread slices next to each other on the baking sheet and spoon the onions over them. Cut the cheese into 1 cm thick slices and place on top. Put the tray in the oven (middle) and bake the onion bread with goat cheese for about 5 minutes, until the cheese runs and turns lightly brown.

74. Bruschetta with herbs

ingredients

- 4 slices of focaccia (or other light country bread)
- 1/2 teaspoon oregano (dried)
- 1/2 teaspoon thyme (dried)
- 1/2 teaspoon marjoram (dried)
- 1 pinch of chili powder

☐ olive oil

preparation

1. For the herb bruschetta, mix the herbs and chili powder together.

2. Briefly toast the bread slices in the preheated oven at 200 ° C (top heat) or in a pan until crispy.

3. Spread the herb mixture on top and generously drizzle the bruschetta with olive oil.

75. Baked avocado baguette

ingredients

- 1 baguette
- 1 avocado
- 5 sun-dried tomatoes (in oil)
- 1/2 bunch of parsley
- 120 g Camembert
- salt
- 1 pinch of cayenne pepper **preparation**

1. For the baked avocado baguette, first cut into the avocado, remove the stone, remove the pulp and mash it with a fork. Cut the sundried tomatoes into small pieces, finely chop the parsley. Cut the camembert into slices. The baguette lengthwise cut through.

2. Mix the avocado with the dried tomatoes, parsley, salt and cayenne pepper and spread on both halves of the baguette. Cover with the cut camembert. Bake in the oven at 180 degrees (fan oven) for 5 to 10 minutes. The baked avocado baguette served warm.

76. Baked baguette with salmon and horseradish

ingredients

- 1 baguette
- 100 g smoked salmon
- 1/2 bunch of dill
- 1/2 cup crème fraîche (alternatively cream cheese)
- 2 tbsp table horseradish
- 80 g Gouda (grated)

salt

- Pepper (from the mill) **preparation**

1. Cut the smoked salmon into fine strips. Chop the dill and mix in a bowl with the sliced salmon, crème fraîche, horseradish and Gouda cheese. Salt and pepper.

2. The baguette cut lengthwise apart.

3. Spread the salmon and horseradish mixture on both halves of the baguette, sprinkle with cheese again if necessary.

4. Bake in a preheated oven at 180-200 ° C (convection) for about 15 minutes.

77. Bruschetta with Tomatoes

ingredients

- 4 slippers (or baguette)
- 2 beefsteak tomatoes (fully ripe)
- 1 spring onion
- 2 anchovies
- 6 tbsp olive oil (cold pressed)
- 1 clove of garlic
- 1 teaspoon oregano (fresh)
- 2 tbsp basil (fresh)

- salt
- pepper

preparation

1. Scald tomatoes with boiling water, rinse with cold water, peel, core and stalk and finely chop the pulp.

2. Pat the anchovy fillets dry and cut into small pieces. Peel and finely dice the garlic.

3. Peel and wash the onion and cut into thin rings.

4. Wash, dry and chop the oregano and basil.

5. Mix all the prepared ingredients, salt and pepper and add the oil.

6. Toast the bread slices (halve the ciabatta beforehand) until golden brown and spread the tomato mixture on top.

7. Serve the bruschetta immediately with tomatoes.

78. Sandwich cake

ingredients

- 12 slice (s) of toast
- 250 g low-fat curd cheese
- 350 g mayonnaise
- 300 ml whipped cream
- 1 can (s) of tuna
- 300 g ham
- 3 eggs (hard-boiled)
  Dill (for sprinkling) **preparation**

1. For the sandwich cake, whip the whipped cream until stiff and mix with the curd and mayonnaise. Divide into three bowls.

2. Mix part of the mixture with tuna and one with ham. Save the rest of the mixture to finish off the sandwich cake.

3. Brush one slice of toast with tuna mixture, place a second slice of toast on top and brush it with ham mixture. Finally, put on another slice of toast and brush with the curd mayonnaise mixture.

4. Place the toast cake in the refrigerator and garnish with eggs and dill before serving.

79. Tuna toast with pesto

ingredients

- 1/2 bell pepper
- 1 can (s) of tuna
- 100 g cream cheese
- Oregano (rubbed)
- salt
- Pepper (from the mill)
- 1/2 onion

4 tbsp pesto

- 8 slice (s) of toast

- 40 g mozzarella **preparation**

1. For the tuna toast with pesto, first prepare the tuna filling. To do this, wash the paprika, remove the stalk and dice. Drain the tuna and mix with the cream cheese, oregano, diced paprika, salt and pepper. Peel the onion, cut in half and cut into very fine strips.

2. First top one half of the toast with pesto, then with the tuna filling, onions and grated mozzarella.

3. Place the second slice of toast on top and bake in the toaster until both halves of the bread are golden brown.

4. Serve the tuna toast with pesto straight away.

80. Bruschette with olive topping

ingredients

- 100 g olive (s) (black)
- 2 pieces of anchovy fillets
- 1 teaspoon of garlic
- 1 tbsp pine nuts
- 4 sage leaves
- 15 pcs. Capers (chopped)
- 2 tbsp olive oil

- rosemary
salt
- pepper
- 1 teaspoon lemon juice **preparation**

1. For the bruschette with olive topping, mix all the ingredients well and season. Brown the bread slices in the oven preheated to 250 ° C for about 4 minutes. Brush with the olive topping and serve immediately.

SALAD RECIPES

81. Panzanella (Tuscan Bread Salad)

Ingredients
- 1 pc. Focaccia (with 300-400g white bread debarked from the previous day)
- 2 onions (or several spring onions)
- 5 tomatoes (preferably fresh from the panicle)
- 1 pc cucumber
- Olives (capers and anchovies as desired)
- 100 ml red wine vinegar
- 200 ml vegetable stock

- 1 bunch of basil (freshly chopped) olive oil
- Sea salt (freshly ground)
- Pepper (freshly ground) **preparation**
2. For the panzanella, cut the stale bread into large cubes and dry on a baking tray overnight. Peel, halve, core the cucumber, cut into slices and lightly season with salt. Quarter the tomatoes and halve again. Cut the peeled onions into fine strips. Mix the red wine vinegar and vegetable stock together. Put the bread cubes in a bowl and drizzle with a little vinegar mixture. Drain excess water from the cucumbers. Mix the cucumber with the onions and tomatoes. Add the rest of the vinegar mixture and the soaked bread. Season with sea salt and pepper from the mill. Mix in capers, olives and chopped anchovies as desired. Finally stir in the olive oil and sprinkle with basil.

82. Tomato bread salad with baked calamaretti

ingredients

For the calamaretti:

- 2 calamaretti
- 100 g of flour
- 1/2 lemon (juice)
- salt
- pepper
- some parsley (chopped)

For the salad:

- 500 g tomatoes
- 200 g ciabatte
- 10 capers (large)
- 1 bunch of basil
- 1 tbsp honey
- 2 tbsp balsamic vinegar
- 3 tbsp olive oil
- salt
- pepper

preparation

3. For the tomato bread salad with baked calamaretti, first pluck the bread into small pieces and season with a little olive oil and salt. Bake in the oven at 200 ° C for about 15 minutes until crispy.

4. Cut the tomatoes into wedges. For the dressing, mix the honey, vinegar and olive oil together well. Halve the caper berries. Mix the tomatoes with the dressing, basil and

capers, stir in the bread and season with salt and pepper.

5. Cut the cleaned calamaretti into thin rings, season with salt, turn in flour and fry in hot sunflower oil until crispy. Season with lemon juice, pepper and parsley before serving.

6. Arrange the salad flat on a plate and spread the calamaretti on top. Serve tomato bread salad with baked calamaretti.

83. White bread salad with mozzarella

ingredients

- 2 packs of light mozzarella (á 125g)
- 150 g white bread (crispy)
- 1 bunch of spring onions
- 1 clove (s) of garlic
- 200 g tomatoes
- 200 g cucumber
- 1 bunch of basil
- 2 tbsp balsamic vinegar
- 3 tbsp walnut oil
- 1 tbsp capers (small)
- salt
- Pepper (freshly ground) **preparation**

1. For the white bread salad, drain and dice the mozzarella. Cut the bread into bite-sized

pieces. Wash and clean the spring onions and cut into narrow strips at a slight angle. Peel and mash the garlic.
2. Wash and clean the tomatoes and cucumber, remove the stem from the tomatoes and cut the vegetables into cubes. Wash the basil, pat dry and pluck the leaves from the stems.
3. Mix the vinegar with salt and pepper, fold in the walnut oil, mix the salad ingredients with the dressing and serve sprinkled with capers.

84. Baked bread salad with dried tomatoes from the hot air fryer

ingredients

- 2 packs of light mozzarella (á 125g)
- 150 g white bread (crispy)
- 1 bunch of spring onions
- 1 clove (s) of garlic
- 200 g tomatoes
- 200 g cucumber
- 1 bunch of basil
- 2 tbsp balsamic vinegar
- 3 tbsp walnut oil
- 1 tbsp capers (small)

- salt
- Pepper (freshly ground)

preparation

1. For the white bread salad, drain and dice the mozzarella. Cut the bread into bite-sized pieces. Wash and clean the spring onions and cut into narrow strips at a slight angle. Peel and mash the garlic.
2. Wash and clean the tomatoes and cucumber, remove the stem from the tomatoes and cut the vegetables into cubes. Wash the basil, pat dry and pluck the leaves from the stems.
3. Mix the vinegar with salt and pepper, fold in the walnut oil, mix the salad ingredients with the dressing and serve sprinkled with capers.

85. Tomato bread salad with fried pulpo

ingredients

For the tomato bread salad:
- 500 g tomatoes
- 1 ciabatte
- 10 olives □ 5 capers
- 1 bunch of basil
- 10 tbsp balsamic vinegar
- 15 tbsp olive oil (good quality)
- 1 teaspoon honey (up to 2 teaspoons)
- salt
- pepper

For the pulpo:
- 1 pulpo (small, approx. 1 kg)

- 1 onion
- 3 bay leaves
- 1 bunch of soup vegetables
- 3 toe (s) of garlic
- salt
- 1 bunch of parsley (small)
- 1 lemon

preparation

1. For the tomato bread salad with fried pulpo, wash the pulpo well, cut the vegetables into cubes and put both together in a saucepan with enough water that the pulpo is barely covered.
2. Cover and cook for about 25 minutes, then simmer again without the lid for 30 to 45 minutes. Pierce with a knife to see if the squid is tender. If so, drain and cut the arms into large pieces.
3. Season the pulpo with a little olive oil and salt, fry it on both sides in a pan or on the grill until crispy. Sprinkle with a little lemon juice and finely chopped parsley.
4. Cut the ciabatta into large cubes, season with a little olive oil and salt and roast in the oven for about 5-10 minutes.

5. Cut the tomatoes into large pieces, the olives and capers into small cubes or slices and mix everything well.
6. Mix the vinegar, honey and olive oil well, mix with the bread and tomatoes, pluck the basil into large pieces and spread over the top.
7. The tomato-bread salad with the fried octopus dish.

86. bread salad

ingredients
- 1 ciabatte
- 1 glass of paprika (grilled)
- 1/2 glass of capers
- 1/2 onion
- 100 g parmesan (grated)
- 50 g prosciutto
- Aceto Balsamico rosso
- oil
- salt
- pepper

preparation

1. For the bread salad, dice the ciabatta and paprika, finely chop the capers and onions and cut the prosciutto into small pieces. Mix the ciabatta with all the ingredients, marinate and serve immediately.

87. Tomato bread salad with baked calamaretti

ingredients *For the calamaretti:* ☐ 2 small squids ☐ 100 g of flour
- 1/2 lemon (juice)
- salt
- pepper
- some parsley (chopped) *For the salad:*
- 500g tomatoes
- 200 g slippers
- 10 capers (large)

- 1 bunch of basil
- 1 tbsp honey
- 2 tbsp balsamic vinegar
- 3 tbsp olive oil
- salt
- pepper

preparation

2. For the tomato bread salad with baked calamaretti, first pluck the bread into small pieces and season with a little olive oil and salt. Bake in the oven at 200 ° C for about 15 minutes until crispy.
3. Cut tomatoes into wedges. For the dressing, mix the honey, vinegar and olive oil together well. Halve the caper berries. Mix the tomatoes with the dressing, basil and capers, stir in the bread and season with salt and pepper.
4. Cut the cleaned calamaretti into thin rings, season with salt, turn in flour and fry in hot sunflower oil until crispy. Season with lemon juice, pepper and parsley before serving.
5. Arrange the salad flat on a plate and spread the calamaretti on top. Serve tomato bread salad with baked calamaretti.

88. Bread salad with beans and peppers

ingredients
- 300 g bread (old)
- 1 pointed pepper (red)
- 10 cherry tomatoes
- 100 g rocket
- 10 parsley leaves
- 10 mint leaves
- 10 fisoles (green)
- 10 fisoles (yellow)
- 1 tbsp maple syrup
- 3 tbsp balsamic vinegar
- 4 tbsp olive oil
- salt
- pepper

preparation

1. Quarter the bell pepper lengthways and remove the stem and seeds. Sear it on all sides in a pan or on the grill.
2. Cook the green beans in plenty of salted water until they are firm to the bite, rinse with cold water and pull apart lengthways, cut the tomatoes in half.
3. Cut the bread into small cubes.
4. Mix the maple syrup, vinegar, olive oil and bread in a bowl; the bread should sear the dressing almost completely and become soft in the process.
5. Add rocket, tomatoes, herbs, green beans and paprika, mix well and season with salt and pepper. Spread on a flat plate and serve immediately.

89. taramosalata

ingredients

- 1/2 loaf (s) of bread (soaked in milk and squeezed out)
- 1 1/2 Glass of Olive Oil
- 1/2 glass of lemon juice
- 160 g tarama (fish roe)
- 3 potatoes (cooked and strained, 4 if necessary)
- Parsley (finely chopped)

preparation

1. Soak the fish roe in a bundle of linen for 1020 minutes in almost boiling water so that

the excess salt in the "tarama" is leached out. Then express it well (or pass it).
2. Mix well with the bread mixture and potatoes.
3. Gradually add olive oil and lemon juice, stirring constantly.
4. Sprinkle the taramosalata with parsley and serve with white bread, pita or raw vegetables.

90. Italian bread salad

ingredients
- 1/2 baguette (diced)
- 100 g salami (spicy)
- 100 g rocket
- 1202 g cherry tomatoes
- 20 ml balsamic vinegar (Bianco)
- olive oil
- sea-salt
- 1 sprig (s) of rosemary
- 50 g parmesan (thinly sliced)
- Pepper

preparation
1. For the Italian bread salad, put some olive oil with a sprig of rosemary in a pan and let it get hot. Roughly slice the salami and fry in the pan until crispy. Then place on crepe paper to cool.
2. Add a little olive oil and the baguette cut into cubes to the hot pan. In the meantime, wash the rocket, remove the stems and season with vinegar, oil, sea salt and pepper.
3. Add the crispy, cooled bread cubes and the salami chips to the rocket and mix everything together well. Finally, mix in some grated Parmesan cheese and sprinkle the rest over the finished Italian bread salad .

91. Crispy bread and cheese salad

ingredients

- 120 g wholemeal rye bread (3 slices)
- 30 g sultanas
- 4 tbsp fruit vinegar
- salt
- pepper
- 4 tbsp safflower oil
- 300 g apples (e.g., elstar, 2 apples)
- 1 ½ bunch radish
- 100 g sliced cheese (e.g., leerdammer, 17% absolute fat)
- 1 bunch flat leaf parsley

Preparation steps

1. Cut the bread into 1 cm cubes and roast them in a non-oiled pan over medium heat for about 4 minutes until crispy. Put on a plate and let cool down.

2. In the meantime, rinse the sultanas with hot water and drain. Mix fruit vinegar with a little salt, pepper and safflower oil to make a salad dressing.

3. Wash the apples, cut each apple from 4 sides towards the center into approximately 5 mm thick slices, cut the slices into cubes. Mix the apple cubes and sultanas with the dressing.

4. Wash, drain and clean the radishes. Put small radish leaves aside; Quarter the radishes.

5. Cut the cheese slices into 2 cm squares. Wash the parsley, shake dry and pluck the leaves.

6. Mix the cheese, parsley and radish leaves, radishes and apple dressing. Season to taste with salt and pepper.

7. Put the lettuce in a well-closing, large food storage container (approx. 1.5 l content) to transport. Put the bread cubes in a smaller food storage container (approx. 500 m capacity) and sprinkle over the cheese and radish salad before serving.

92. Cevapcici in flatbread

Ingredients
- 1 kg minced meat (mixed beef/lamb or beef/pork)
- 1 large onion
- 3 cloves of garlic a
- little fresh parsley
- 1 tbsp olive oil
- 1 tbsp salt
- 3 tsp paprika powder
- 3 tsp pepper, finely ground
- Flatbread
- salad ☐ ajvar
- hot peppers

Preparation

3. The onion is finely grated (not chopped), the garlic cloves are pressed, the parsley finely chopped. The minced meat is mixed well with onion, garlic, parsley and the other ingredients so that the spices are evenly distributed.
4. Now you form thumb-thick cevapcici, about 7 cm long. The use of the Cevapomaker is suitable here, with which you can form seven Cevapcici in one course. *Grilling*
   2. The grill is prepared for direct grilling over medium heat. The cevapcici are placed on the hot grid, turned after 3 - 4 minutes and grilled on the other side. Then the cevapcici is removed from the grill and we prepare the flatbreads. The flatbread is topped with salad and 6 - 7 cevapcici are placed on top. Spread 2 - 3 tablespoons of ajar over it and place two peppers on top.

93. Fluffy Protein Bread With Nutri-Plus

Ingredients
- 90 g neutral Nutri-Plus protein powder
- 200 g Cashews
- 200 g linseed
- 500 g Unsweetened soya yogurt
- 150 ml of water
- 100 g Sunflower seeds
- 1 pck. baking powder
- 1/2 tsp salt

Preparation
1. First put the cashews, linseed and protein powder in a blender and chop everything together to a coarse flour.
2. Then pour the soy yogurt, water, baking soda and salt into a bowl and add the cashew protein powder mixture.
3. Third Stir everything into a smooth dough and fill it into a baking paper-lined form.
4. Let the dough shell for about 10-15 minutes. In time, you can preheat the oven to 175 ° C.
5. Bake the bread for about 60 minutes. To make sure it's really baked through, do the stick test.
6. Allow cooling, to taste delicious and then let taste.

94. Colorful layered salad

Ingredients
- iceberg lettuce
- tomatoes
- ¾ cans of corn
- medium cucumbers
- yellow pepper
- 2-3 red onions
- chicken breasts (about 0.5 kg)
- seasoning for peas and chicken
- 2-3 pieces of bread
- seasoning for toasts
- Butter and oil for frying
- Herb sauce

preparation:
1. Cut the chicken into small pieces, sprinkle with gyros and chicken, the season in the fridge for 1-2 hours.
2. Layer the salad in layers. We tear the lettuce and put the dishes on the bottom. Cut the tomatoes into halves or slices. We drain the corn. Peel cucumbers and cut into halves or slices. Then cut the peppers into strips. Cut the red onions into quarters of the slices.
3. We heat oil and fry chicken.
4. Cut the bread into small cubes, warm up the butter in a pan and pour the sliced bread on them. Fry until golden brown, sprinkle with a toast to the end of frying.
5. We prepare herbal sauce according to the recipe on the packaging and pour the whole salad before serving.

95. Caprese sandwich

Ingredients
- 2 slices or slices of bread that are consistent
- Sliced fresh tomato
- Slices of fresh mozzarella
- 1 handful of fresh basil leaves
- 1 tablespoon pesto sauce or a dash of extra virgin olive oil
- Salt and pepper

Preparation
1. Place the slices of bread on a plate and sprinkle with olive oil or spread with a little pesto sauce.
2. We put the tomato in slices, pepper the tomato and place the slices of mozzarella and the basil leaves washed and dried. Cover with the other slice of bread.
3. We serve at the moment, freshly made, so that it does not get wet and deteriorate

96. Baked eggplant parmesan in the leaf pan

ingredients

- Cut 3 medium-sized eggplants or 5 small 1/2 inch circles
- eggs, beaten
- 1 cup of Italian seasoned breadcrumbs
- Extra virgin olive oil for drizzling
- 1/2 glass of marinara sauce
- Cut 5-6 tomatoes into thick slices
- balls of buffalo mozzarella, halved (see picture above)
- 1/4 cup grated parmesan
- about 15 fresh basil leaves **preparation**

1. Oven preheats to 425 F.
2. Sprinkle the eggplant in the egg, breadcrumb, and spread thinly on the sheet pan. Bake for another 15 minutes. Remove sheet pan and cool down to 350 F. Flip over each eggplant but still don't return to the oven.
3. Layer a little sauce over each aubergine. Place one slice of tomato on top of that. Sprinkle a small amount of salt over each tomato. Place a half-round of mozzarella buffalo on top of each tomato. Adjust for 15 minutes to the oven at 350 F.
4. Switch the oven on broil on top after 15 minutes have passed. Broil for 3 minutes, or until the cheese is golden brown and melty. Keep a close watch so the cheese is not burning.
5. Remove the sheet pan and brush with parmesan on each eggplant, adding a basil leaf to top. Love it!

97. Grilled Eggplant Sandwich

Ingredient

- 1 medium eggplant (or 2 small zucchini)
- 1 to 2 tablespoons low-sodium soy sauce (use wheat-free soy sauce if you are gluten sensitive)
- 1 tablespoon balsamic vinegar
- 8 large, thick slices of whole-grain bread or gluten-free bread
- 1 roasted red pepper, sliced
- 1 large roasted garlic head
- 4 teaspoons of Dijon mustard (optional)
- 4 leaves of red lettuce **Preparation**

1. Cut the eggplant diagonally into slices 1/4 inch (6 mm).
2. Brush the eggplant slices with soy sauce and roast them on a grill or iron skillet seasoned over medium-high heat for 2 to 4 minutes on each side until they are soft and lightly browned.
3. Remove them from the pan and sprinkle with vinegar. Set them aside. Toast the bread, if desired and spread 2 to 4 cloves of garlic in the lower slice, add a layer of grilled eggplant, folding the soft pieces to fit in the slice of bread.
4. Top with slices of roasted red pepper and lettuce. Spread mustard over the top slice of bread, if desired, then complete the sandwich and serve.

98. Herb egg bread with tomato cream

ingredients

- 2 slice (s) of black bread
- 1 spring onion (small, washed, cut into rings)
- Cress (for sprinkling)
- 2 tbsp butter (for frying)

For the tomato cream:

- 4 tbsp cream cheese
- 6 tbsp tomato paste

- salt
- Pepper (from the mill)

For the herb egg dish:

- 4 eggs
- 1 shot of mineral water
- 1/2 bunch of parsley (washed, finely chopped) ☐ 1/2 bunch of chives (washed, cut into rolls)
- 1 handful of sprouts (of your choice, e.g. red cabbage sprouts)
- salt
- Pepper (from the mill)
- 1 pinch nutmeg (grated) **preparation**

1. For herb egg bread, beat the eggs with tomato cream, sprinkle with mineral water and season well with salt, pepper and nutmeg. Stir in herbs.

2. Melt the butter in a pan. As soon as the butter starts to bubble, pour the herb-egg mixture into the pan and let it set slowly, stirring again and again. As soon as the egg dish is firm at the bottom but still slightly runny at the top, remove the pan from the heat and set aside.

3. For the tomato cream, roughly mix the cream cheese with 2 tablespoons of tomato paste, season with salt & pepper. Halve the bread slices to taste and brush with 2 tablespoons of tomato paste each, then spread the tomato cream on top. "Pick up" herb egg dishes with a fork and spread on the bread.

4. Sprinkle herb egg bread with tomato cream with cress and spring onion and serve.

99. Mediterranean toasts

Ingredients 2 portions

- 1/2 can chickpeas
- 1 handful arugula (approximately 10 leaves)
- 2 slices bread (better field)
- 1 expert tomato
- Acheto
- Olive
- Salt

Preparation
1. Cut the tomato into slices, not very thin. Cook them in a pan with a drizzle of olive. Do

not remove them, only turn them when cooked on one side. Add a splash of ache to. Reservation.

2. Mash the chickpea and a little olive. You can process it, but with a fork, it goes well. If you want salt, I made this recipe without salt and it was great.
3. Wash the arugula leaves
4. Brush the slices of bread with olive and toast
5. Spread the bread with the chickpea. Above the chickpea, arrange some tomato slices, and on them the arugula. Finish with a thread of olive oil.

100. Tramezzini with egg and anchovies

Ingredients

- 12 slices of tramezzini bread (soft, juicy white bread without rind)
- 6 eggs (hard-boiled and thinly sliced)
- 12 anchovy fillets (inlaid)
- 200 g mayonnaise (homemade if possible)

Preparation

1. Brush the bread slices generously with mayonnaise. The top half of the bread with half of the egg slices. Place the drained anchovy fillets on top and top with the remaining egg slices. Put the remaining bread slices on top and cut diagonally into two triangles.

CONCLUSION

Enjoy the smell of freshly baked bread in your kitchen - make bread or cook it with bread. From homemade sourdough, to stuffed holiday bread, from sandwiches to bread soup ... Whether it's whole meal bread, olive bread or stuffed bread, whether it's peasant bread, Weckerl or panini, whether it's black or white, here you will find many bread and pastry recipes. There are also useful tips and tricks to ensure the success of your bread. Vary your favorite bread with new spices, herbs, nuts or seeds.

www.ingramcontent.com/pod-product-compliance
Lightning Source LLC
Chambersburg PA
CBHW070356120526
44590CB00014B/1154